Underwater World

CRABS

By Ryan Nagelhout

Gareth Stevens
Publishing

Please visit our website, www.garethstevens.com. For a free color catalog of all our high-quality books, call toll free 1-800-542-2595 or fax 1-877-542-2596.

Library of Congress Cataloging-in-Publication Data

Nagelhout, Ryan.
Crabs / Ryan Nagelhout.
p. cm. — (Underwater world)
Includes index.
ISBN 978-1-4339-8568-3 (pbk.)
ISBN 978-1-4339-8569-0 (6-pack)
ISBN 978-1-4339-8567-6 (library binding)
1. Crabs—Juvenile literature. I. Title.
QL444.M33N336 2013
595.3'86—dc23
2012019201

First Edition

Published in 2013 by
Gareth Stevens Publishing
111 East 14th Street, Suite 349
New York, NY 10003

Editor: Ryan Nagelhout
Designer: Katelyn Londino

Photo credits: Cover, p. 1 © iStockphoto.com/Tammy616; p. 5 Colin Keates/Dorling Kindersley/Getty Images; pp. 7, 24 (shell) peter_krejzl/Shutterstock.com; pp. 9, 24 (claws) Jason Patrick Ross/Shutterstock.com; p. 11 © iStockphoto.com/tunart; p. 13 Photofish/Shutterstock.com; p. 15 Birute Vijeikiene/Shutterstock.com; p. 17 Ingram Publishing/Thinkstock.com; p. 19 CHRISTOPHE SIMON/AFP/Getty Images; p. 21 davidpstephens/Shutterstock.com; p. 23 MindStorm/Shutterstock.com; p. 24 (dinosaur) Hemera/Thinkstock.com.

Printed in the United States of America

CPSIA compliance information: Batch #CW13GS: For further information contact Gareth Stevens, New York, New York at 1-800-542-2595.

Contents

Old Animals 4
Claws and Legs 8
Kinds of Crabs. 16
Words to Know 24
Index. 24

Crabs once lived with dinosaurs!

They have a hard skin.
This is called their shell.

They often have
two sharp hands.
These are its claws.

They have many legs.

Most crabs walk
side to side.
Others walk like us!

They will eat almost
anything small!
They eat plants
and animals.

They come in many shapes and sizes. There are over 4,400 different kinds!

They can live
in many places.

Some are blue.
They can live in the sea.

Others are red.
They can live on land.

Words to Know

claws

dinosaur

shell

Index

claws 8

kinds 16

legs 10

shell 6